AMAZING ANIMAL PARTS

Animal Tails

by Mari Schuh

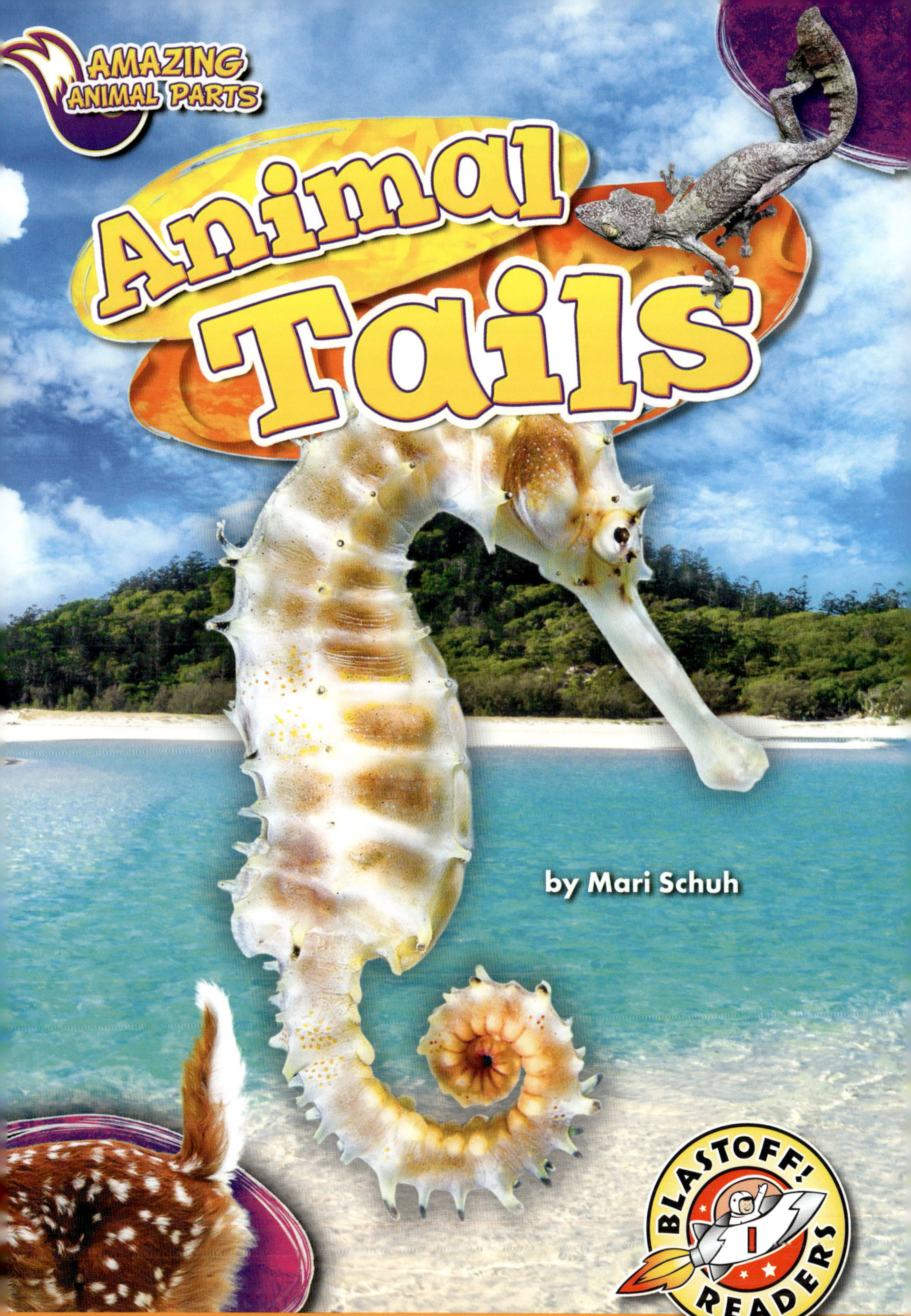

BELLWETHER MEDIA • MINNEAPOLIS, MN

Blastoff! Readers are carefully developed by literacy experts to build reading stamina and move students toward fluency by combining standards-based content with developmentally appropriate text.

Level 1 provides the most support through repetition of high-frequency words, light text, predictable sentence patterns, and strong visual support.

Level 2 offers early readers a bit more challenge through varied sentences, increased text load, and text-supportive special features.

Level 3 advances early-fluent readers toward fluency through increased text load, less reliance on photos, advancing concepts, longer sentences, and more complex special features.

★ **Blastoff! Universe**

Reading Level

Blastoff! Beginners — Grade K

Blastoff! Readers — Grades 1–3

Blastoff! Discovery — Grade 4

This edition first published in 2024 by Bellwether Media, Inc.

Library of Congress Cataloging-in-Publication Data

LC record for Animal Tails available at: https://lccn.loc.gov/2023039763

Editor: Rebecca Sabelko Designer: Andrea Schneider

Printed in the United States of America, North Mankato, MN.

Table of Contents

Many Different Tails

Animals use their tails in many ways. Tails come in many shapes and sizes!

Fluffy Tails

Arctic foxes have long, fluffy tails. Their tails are called brushes.

Arctic foxes use
their tails as blankets.
They stay warm
in their cold home!

Tails Help Animals

hide

hold on

move

Leaf Tails

Geckos are lizards.
Some live in forests.

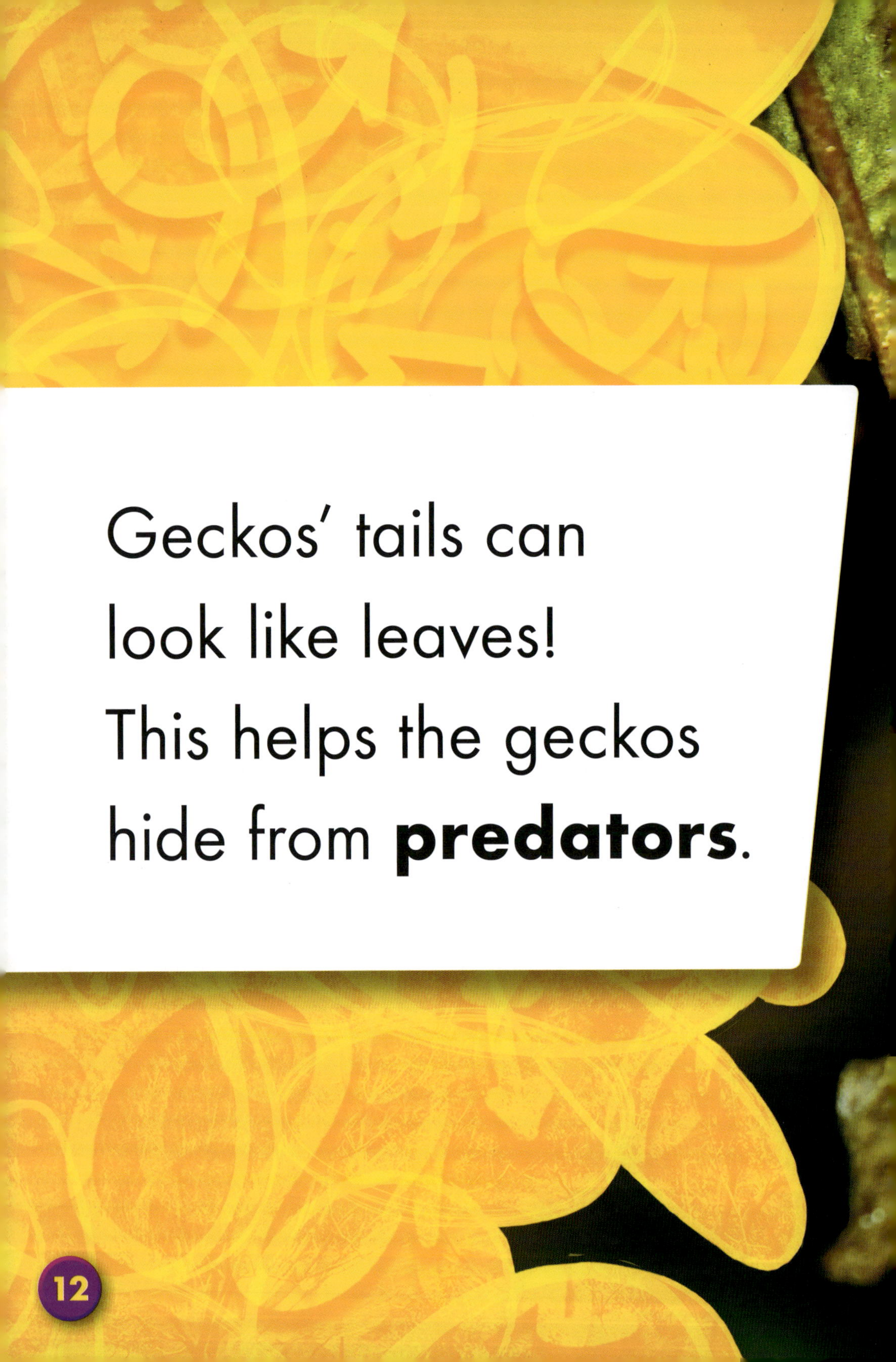

Geckos' tails can look like leaves! This helps the geckos hide from **predators**.

predator

Curly Tails

Sea horses are fish. But they do not swim well in ocean **currents**.

Their **prehensile** tails **wrap** around plants. Sea horses do not float away!

More Prehensile Tails!

binturong

red howler monkey

Virginia opossum

Tail Warning

White-tailed deer use their tails as **warnings**. They lift their tails when danger is near.

Other deer see their white tail fur. It is time to run!

Glossary

currents

movements of water in an ocean that happen over and over

warnings

actions that tell others that danger is near

predators

animals that hunt other animals for food

wrap

to fold or wind around something

prehensile

able to wrap around and hold on

To Learn More

AT THE LIBRARY

Culliford, Amy. *Tail*. New York, N.Y.: Crabtree Publishing Company, 2022.

Davidson, Rose. *Animal Tails*. Washington, D.C.: National Geographic Kids, 2023.

Griffin, Mary. *Whose Tail Is That?* New York, N.Y.: Gareth Stevens Publishing, 2024.

ON THE WEB

FACTSURFER

Factsurfer.com gives you a safe, fun way to find more information.

1. Go to www.factsurfer.com.
2. Enter "animal tails" into the search box and click 🔍.
3. Select your book cover to see a list of related content.

Index

The images in this book are reproduced through the courtesy of: Miroslav Halama, front cover (gecko); Frolova_Elena, front cover (sea horse); Imagebroker/ Alamy, front cover (deer tail), pp. 18-19; Sina Ettmer Photography, front cover (landscape background); Eric Isselee, p. 3 (scorpion tail); nizha2, p. 3 (lemur); Henk Bogaard, pp. 4-5; Alexey Seafarer, pp. 6-7; L-N, pp. 8-9; Anna Veselova, p. 9 (hide); jeanyanitha, p. 9 (hold on); Justin Berken, p. 9 (move); jez_bennett, pp. 10-11; Damian Ryszawy, pp. 12-13; Monika Surzin, p. 13 (predators); Vojce, pp. 14-15; WhitcombeRD, pp. 16-17; phichak, p. 17 (binturong); Salparadis, p. 17 (red howler monkey); Jay Ondreicka, p. 17 (Virginia opossum); georgesanker.com/ Alamy, pp. 20-21; GuadiLab, p. 22 (currents); Justlight, p. 22 (predators); kary.feer, p. 22 (prehensile); SuJo Studios, p. 22 (warnings); Ery Azmeer, p. 22 (wrap).